Metamorphosis

JOAN I. SIEGEL

Metamorphosis

Copyright © 2017 by Joan I. Siegel

All rights reserved. No part of this book may be reproduced or transmitted in any form or by any means without written permission of the author.

Author photo credit: Emily Solonche
Cover design by Jack Heller

Library of Congress Control Number: 2017932028

ISBN: 978-0-9915772-1-7

Published by Shabda Press
Pasadena, CA 91107
www.shabdapress.com

Acknowledgements

Some poems listed below may appear with different titles and in altered form since publication.

Poet Lore . . . . After Divorcing
The Bridge . . . . Last Light
Hawaii Pacific Review . . . . Black Cat
Chautauqua . . . . Playing Clair de Lune on My Mother's Birthday
Comstock Review . . . . Last Morning of My Mother

Contents

PART I 1
Duet 3
A Mother's Death 4
Another Letter to My Daughter's Mother 5
Childless 6
April 7
Connotations 8
Dying Humming Bird 9
Far, Far Away 10
Waiting 11
The Armchair 12
Anonymous: *Young Woman on Her Deathbed* 13
Poem 14
Survival 15
The Dreamer and the Dreamed 16
After Hours in the Gallery 18
When George Learned His Friend Died 19
Cancer 20
Nick's Dog 21

PART II 23
Metaphor 25
Beech Tree in Winter 26
Lost Rooms 27
Autograph Album 28
Auto Accident 29
Vanishing Point 30
The Sea 31
Before Divorcing 32
Ritual 33

Rain 34
Everglades Afternoon 35

PART III 37
Boy on a Bicycle 39
To One Who Would Be Zeus 40
Koan 41
Photograph: Wanda Landowska (1944) 42
The Poem of the Future 43
Smile 44
The Soul's Provenance 45
Taking the Measure of Things 46
Thoughts on a December Afternoon 47
A Mother's Vigil 48
Woman without Child 49
Unreeling 50
Vermeer: The Lacemaker 51
Vigilance 52
Going to Sleep 53
At the End 54
No Rain in the Forecast 55
Two White Swans 56
The Wedding 57

PART IV 59
Growing up in America 61
Blue Heron 63
Fog 64
Vanishing Point 65
Gaea Speaks 66
Ghost 67
Heaven 68
Homesickness 69

PART V 71
Your Life without You. 73
The Blessings of the Grandchild 74
October 75
Last Light 76
Spring 77
Balancing. 78
Improvisation 79
Interim 80
Keeping Her Company 81
What I Would Give Up 83
On Your Fifty-Seventh Birthday 84
Homesickness 85

PART I

Duet

After he died
she wore his old bathrobe to bed
fingering the frayed
pockets knotting
stray threads unknotting
them as if solving
the puzzle of death questioning
him in the darkening room
before sleep answering
in his voice just as the bird
whose mate is long gone sings
both choruses.

A Mother's Death

She takes with her
the rest of the story—
what you will never know
about yourself. How
you moved inside her, rubbing
up against her ribs. The ocean
of your breath in her ear
whenever she held you.
What you looked like
when you awoke. How
rooms filled whenever
you were gone from the house.

Another Letter to My Daughter's Mother

When I look at her
am I seeing you?

When I look at her smile
is it her father's smile?

What gesture is her grandmother's?
her great Aunt's?

Her cheeks bloom like Chinese roses.
her eyes are black lakes.

They have drunk the sun all day.
they give back moonlight,

Stars. They keep
what can't be given back.

Childless

Too early, this November snow
crests outside   windows

buries the wood pile. It isn't yet
the shortest day of the year.

Willows sag like old women
heavy as the leaden sky

bearing down on the house.

April

This afternoon my friend leaves work early
to look for her old dog who wandered from
the house and will die without his insulin shot.

In the upstairs bedroom, her lover is dying
from cancer. My friend may or may not find
the dog crouched beneath the porch waiting.

Her lover will not last the month. The dog may
turn up dead in a farmer's field. Meanwhile,
on the knotted buds, rain.

Connotations

Words burst from your mouth
like seeds from ripe milkweed,
silk threads that drift earthward
to root and flower.

Some are flat like *mat*.
Some are round like *globe*.
Some are sharp like *scissors*.

Others are shiny and red
as the apple that crisps your tongue,
snaps between your teeth
and tastes of leafy orange days.

When trees rain on your shoes,
blackbirds storm overhead
and it seems you have lived forever

under the sun.

Dying Humming Bird

It might have been a leaf
blown from a tree
the way it curled into itself
beside the wild lupine.

Emerald light
you could touch.
Aerialist fallen from the sky

onto the tarmac.
Its wings singing
fiercely as the heart
in its splintered cage.

Far, Far Away

They scan the night, sifting
for particles of dark
matter precious as gold dust:

Star clusters 13,000 light-
years from my window
where the long ago child I was

scanned shadows the full moon
stained on my bedroom wall,
and free-falling, I dropped

from the shelf of sleep
through deepest night,
whirling alongside galaxies

of planets and suns so far
from home, afraid of the dark
lapping at my feet, I swam up

to first light.

Waiting

We are all waiting for the same thing

even as we turn on the radio
turn it off
turn it on again

even as we invent new words
speak them
unspeak them
hear them sucked back to air

even as we read to our children
put them to bed
wake them for school
fill a glass of milk

even as we forget last night's
dreams with our morning tea
lace our shoes
unlace them at the end of the day

even as the rain falls
the clouds dry up
our mouths fill with dust

The Armchair

The armchair does not sing.
It does not play violin.
It waits—

For the old woman
to sit back and sigh
a long sigh
and remember.

For the schoolgirl
to fall asleep over
her school books
and dream.

For the cat
to drape herself like a curtain
and nap.

For the widower
to listen to Brahms quartets
and grieve.

For the moon
to fill the armchair's
lap.

Anonymous: *Young Woman on Her Deathbed*

(17th Century)

After they have closed her eyes,
lifted her from the bed
the bed will not give up its own.

That's the way with the dead
who stay behind—
under the bedcovers, fingers
blue against white linen,
head weighing into the pillow,
sheets creased warm
with the body's smell.

Even the covers seem to rise
and fall out of breath.

Poem

Because I had a bad dream last night
the sky was grey as a hammer.
I thought I heard the telephone ring.
It was a key falling.
Once. Then twice.
All night the air was sweet with rainwater.
I thought I heard a cat cry.
It was a twisted branch sliding down the roof.
That happened once before.
Then the sky lay down beside me.
The sun curled up in a cloud.
The telephone rang.
Once. Then twice.
I thought it was my daughter calling.
It was a bird singing in a twisted branch.

Survival

*Three Haikus for our Chinese Daughter
abandoned at a railway station in
Zhezhiang Province, (1994)*

i.

Peony sealed tight
against savage winter teeth
impenetrable.

ii.

Sun stirs pallid roots
warming petals one by one:
pink mouth for singing.

iii.

Wounds close over
layer by layer, you grow
toward us in the light.

The Dreamer and the Dreamed

Do you ever wonder
if the person you dreamed about
knows it?

Do you carry him off
at midnight, hold him
hostage to your sleep?

Do you make love?
Go for a walk?
Bake bread?

Maybe he falls off the bed
and reappears on the stairs humming
a Bach cantata.

Later, he says everything
you've always wanted to hear
about your beauty

your grace
your wit
how artfully you play the violin.

He pulls a wrinkled paper
from his pocket and reads
a poem…

I'm ill at numbers.
I have not art
to reckon my groans.

And when you see him again at work,
does he look at you meaningfully?
Talk about losing his bearings?
How he can't account for lost time?

After Hours in the Gallery

Paring knife raised
turnip pinched between
two fingers, she looks
at the girl pouring milk

the girl ironing
the girl sewing
the girl scrubbing the floor
the girl carrying bricks.

She hears the spill of milk
hiss of the hot iron
prick of the needle
scratch of the brush
drag of the feet.

Hands coarse as hopsacking
pale as root vegetables soaking
in the earthenware bowl at her feet.
She drops the knife. The turnip
slips, splashes in cold water.

She unknots her apron.
Jumps out of the frame.

When George Learned His Friend Died

Fifty years was the continent
we started from together. We walked
in step for a while, then you went
your way.

           I followed
my feethow they took me
from one sunrise to another,
one darkness to another.

           I learned to balance
on the rim of darkness and light,
knowing all things fold into each other
like faces of the moon.

           At the vanishing point,
you slipped away…
                  with your take on our story.

Cancer

When it had spread to the lungs
had etched its way into the other organs
carving out the living tissue, it sculpted
the corpse he was to become. All the while
his wife and children wept silently
even as they carried soup to his bedside
and propped him on pillows, telling him
news of the day and wiping dribble
from his chin and later discarding
the mattress and bedclothes with
the body's waste while they
watched the skin stretch tighter
over the bones and tendons, the eyes
cast deeper inside the skull, the chisled
form emerge as from stone.

Nick's Dog

All the while,
the dog, part shepherd-part lab, watched
at the bed, rushing from one side
to another when he turned and tracking
him to the toilet and back, licking wildly
his hands and face and the few times
the ambulance carried him away
for a week or two, the dog howled
his wolf's howl, then whimpered
on the front stoop all day, guarding
his bed all night until he came back
and finally when Nick went off
to the funeral home for the viewing,
they let the dog come along,
but he broke loose,
jumped in beside his man
and when at last they could quiet him,
he sat, *good dog*,
keeping watch like Argos

PART II

Metaphor

Some things are just what they are:
blue herons flying over a pond at dawn.

if they were anything else

it would be music
scored for solo voice.

Beech Tree in Winter

Wearing
its coppery leaves
like an old woman
in her faded housedress
who waits up long after
the family
has gone to bed.

All night
she keeps watch.

Memory settles
quiet as snow
around the house.

Lost Rooms

You do not shut the book
you are reading, finish
your tea, wash the cup before

like some ancient people
whose shards are unearthed centuries
later and one walks in their dust
wondering what they were thinking
at the end.

How many rooms
do you vanish from
in a lifetime?

If you force the door
open, can you sit again
in your armchair by the window,
finish your tea, pick up
the thread of the story?

Autograph Album

Class of '25

(Go little album far and near
To all my friends who are so dear.
Let them each sign a page
That I may read in my old age.)

In the sunlight between
wars, they flit among
water-color pages
like butterflies dusting
hydrangea. Their words swell
with promise: tight as buds
blossoming, the warm surge
on midnight sheets. At day's
end, they race out school doors
to the playing field. *Fly away Jack*
Fly away Jill. A matter of luck
not getting tagged out. Across
the new millennium, the winners
push their walkers.

Auto Accident

Another turn of machinery
more or less of steel unmeshed
and glass ground into bone
and I would be borne
and buried peeling off skin
and bits of lashes down
in the dark where you cannot
touch my face.

        I cannot share my grave
with you and if I could? We would grow
bored of the night
      of sleeping soft belly to bone.

In time you would stretch,
want to rise and take a walk,
smoke a cigarette

and when you couldn't
what would we do
but sit back
watch ourselves fall away
cell by cell
unmade.

Vanishing Point

The sun warmed green pulls
taut along the riptide
to a sandy point of gulls

that edge of earth
where sailors feared to fall:
black space of moons and fire
airless and dry.

Fearless
I step off the shelf of green
into grey descend

through the sea's dark forests
through pearls and silvered fish
to cold and night while the sun
burns gold above.

I sleep on a bed of chalked bones
forgetting the sound
of plovers' wings.

The Sea

breaks against my legs
gathering up its own

white fingers reach
between my toes
dragging shells and grass

blanched stones roll
and grate in foam

only vast un-peopled space
and lonely caves carved
in lime

somewhere
beyond this grey waste

of thunder and phantom bones
is home where voices of green earth
call to me.

The sea washes up
and gently tugs.

Before Divorcing

is disengagement
imperceptible
as the peeling off
of the moon's old face.
Slow and quiet
as the pulling away of tides:
without tension except
at the tear.

What if continents floated together again
crashing into each other
or the moon reached back
for its face? Would it be easeful
meshing or a jagged intersection
of edges?

Ritual

Each morning at six,
our neighbor's dog
climbs up the hill
to our back door to feast
on scraps of food
we've saved for him.
We hear his panting
before we see him
waiting there. His
threadbare coat
encrusted with scabs
where black fur used
to grow. His eyes are
rheumy and sad. They
seem to say, *my time
is almost up but this is mine.*
He chews the food, then
licks the dish and sits
awhile to think before
he stands on shaky legs
and shuffles downhill.

Rain

It's one of those wet and leafy
September afternoons
when gargoyles seem
to have sprouted on trees
draining rainwater to ferns below
and already maple leaves
have turned garnet and gold
littering the road and I am not ready
for changes of any kind:
just the rain falling
through branches
just the rain.

Everglades Afternoon

Swamp thick,
this afternoon sleeps
beside the river of grass
where alligators slap
the mud, turtles dream
slow dreams.

An ibis sways
on one red leg.

Here is time
thick as pond apples
hanging over
seagrass

time slow as coral
snakes uncoiling
in limestone pits,
slow as strangling figs,
slow as the white oak's
death.

PART III

Boy on a Bicycle

A boy passes me on a bicycle this morning
going the opposite way. When I reach the end
of the road, I turn around. Now we are both
travelling the same direction or so it seems.
He is out of sight. He might have turned left
at the railroad bed or right onto the main road
two miles ahead. I wonder is he headed for a friend's
house or just out for a ride. Did his father
beat him this morning and his mother
looked up with sadness as he passed
the kitchen window? Or maybe he has
 a different father who is out back splitting
wood and his mother died of cancer two
winters ago. He is just a boy on a bicycle
who passed me on the road some minutes
ago and should have passed out of memory
by now, but I hold him back from his destination
wondering about chance, why he passed me
at just that time and place an what is happening
right now that may never happen again in
just the same way which will change his life
or mine forever.

To One Who Would Be Zeus

I never thought you made a convincing king of the Gods
even with your grey beard and Agean color eyes or
your exploits in the woods chasing would-be nymphs:
but it was the pantheon of children on your knee
that made me think there might be something to it
the way all these years later they come back to you,
singing bearing gifts and again and again gifts.

Koan

It is said we have two faces.
   The one we see in the mirror.
   The one we had before
   we were born.

      The one
   in the mirror we recognize
   until we look too long
   and it loses meaning.

   The other face
   looks out at the world
   when the sun spills
     itself on the sea.
       When we sit listening.

Photograph: Wanda Landowska (1944)

Soceress in black dress & white hands.

The cat beside her
black & white.
Eyes taut as harp strings.

He peers into the black hammers
silver wires
music precise as cat feet.

Head bowed to the ivories
she conjures Bach
with her right hand

while deep in the black keys,
her left hand summons
all the light of this world.

The Poem of the Future

The poem of the future will be scribed with ink
pressed from pine smoke and soot
and the gall nuts of trees or dried hawthorn
soaked and boiled in water and wine.

The poem of the future will be scribed by quill
and the poet's white shirt and hands stained
squid-black, his finger indented where
the pen pressed hard upon the knuckle.

The poem of the future will be an epic of the past.
It will have twenty-four books about the great deeds
of small men and the nefarious deeds of great ones
and the unsung deeds of the unsung.

The poem of the future will be chanted
in the town square where blind men
will sing it to their children and their children's
children will carve it in stone.

Smile

In her school pictures
my daughter's smile
slips into place:

a tight seam straining
the edges.

Her eyes say,
This is counterfeit.

The Soul's Provenance

Some say it is conceived with the body.
shapeless as a conscience, it dwells
apart from the mind and senses
in its own room, dark and
cramped as an anchorite's cell
where it thinks its own thoughts,
keeps its own counsel. When
finally the house is razed, it
floats away like dust.

Others say it takes up residence
at birth: white haired and sage
as a grandmother in a rocking chair
waiting for you to climb up on her
lap for advice.

But I have also heard that it thrives
among the elements in sunlight and air.
So various and expansive, it lives outside
its house, enfolding mind and body
in a web spun loose as the wood spider's
that bends and flexes, gives way to the wind.

Taking the Measure of Things

In college we used the slide rule
to measure inside the atom,
invisible things.

           We measured
in moles. My teacher said
she never saw a mole,
 but like God, she believed
 it must be.

Later I took the measure
of darkness on earth
and there I found God
rending his white beard.

Thoughts on a December Afternoon

The flight of snow geese
their longing for another place
is like my own longing
to put off darkness.

Years ago my father clawed
the bed sheets searching
for a light switch because
inside his brain it had grown
dark. Only a Chopin etude
from the living room quieted
his hands.

After all is it possible
to take along one thing?
music?
sunlight on white wings?

A Mother's Vigil

    for Emily

When you are sick with fever
I lie in your bed awake
delirious
that the night will grow flames
that flames will lick your feet
singe your hair
scorch the red heart of you.
I keep watch all night
ready to swallow fire
beat it back with my fists
smother it under my belly
and burn for you
all the long hours
until the cold sun
breaks the dark window.

Woman without Child

In the waiting room
Other women blossom in their bellies.
Their breasts fill.

Other women's children
call you Auntie.

Alone in your house
you feel your breasts shrink
the bones of your hips
snap shut.

Unreeling

When I unreeled
all the home movies
our parents were
seventeen years dead
each reel sputtering
on the ground, spinning
away those days of the family
when all that would happen
hadn't happened yet
and my mother is still young
wearing a blue sundress
and an ambiguous smile
scolding my father as she sits
on the porch of the summer hotel
because she doesn't want
her picture taken and already
beneath the words
is the stone
where anger is honed
so my father clowns at himself
in the camera's eye, then turns
toward the cold spring-fed pool
where my sister looks away
while I smile my silliest smile
as if smiling long and hard enough
will break the spell, heal
the bruised look in her eyes,
dull the sharp edge
of my mother's tongue.

Vermeer: The Lacemaker

Light shines through her face
warms her hands
lacing silk.

The absolute stillness
as though it were
an act of devotion:

how a woman's fingers
tweezes a splinter from a child's foot
touches a man's body

shuts the eyes of the dead.

Vigilance

Among those wide-hipped women
hips slow as palm fronds swagging

in the summer heat, breasts like melons
joggling beneath their shirts:

Here run the children, shouting unafraid
in the sweat and laughter of their mothers' smell.

On the savannas, elephant mothers
and great aunts, their gray broadsides

walling the young. Whale mothers
breaching waves, babies arcing behind.

When I pass her fawns at the edge
of the woods, she eyes me, ready

to herd them back toward the denser growth,
eat their excreta to disguise their smell.

Going to Sleep

Why do we say we are going to sleep
as if to the movies or Milwaukee
and we are standing around
in the busy terminal of our minds
where all the voices of the day
mill about to catch the train
that slows down for us to hop aboard
drop our suitcases on the platform
taking along a hat which blows out
the window and lands on yesterday's
newspaper printed in a language
we no longer speak here in this place
where we end up in our underwear
making a brilliant speech in the town
square which everyone applauds wildly
before chasing us out of town.

At the End

She was afraid
to let go of all
she'd ever known.
After 89 years,
she couldn't just
let it slip
from her shoulders
like a threadbare coat
give it back
to her mother—say
I can't use this anymore
longing to crawl into her arms
one last time

Where could she go without it?
No voice speaking her name.
No hand reaching.

No Rain in the Forecast

White hot sky leans down
on ash trees. Seared leaves fold up:
unused umbrellas

Two White Swans

"It's in the imagination
   with which you perceive
        this world…" (Mary Oliver)

The first of December
and two white swans rise
from the lake, their heavy
wings thumping
like heartbeats.

Such strength
could crack my bones.

Still, the power of their wings,
the heavy drumming
in the morning's quiet
the white bodies skimming
make me stay, not needing
to be elsewhere, knowing
anything else.

The Wedding

Even in this imperfect place
geese mate for life and mill
upon the lake awaiting
whatever pinches beneath the wing
to urge them elsewhere, it's such
a momentous event: that boisterous
passage across the evening sky.
We look up wanting to go with them.

We need the ritual, its rubric
and solemnity.
We need the bounty of flowers,
food and wine. We need to sing
and dance noisily in the village
square, throw up our arms and
shout, scare off death:

and afterward
such quiet descending on our sleep
like pairs of folded wings.

PART IV

Growing up in America

1946

We grew up
on the other side
of the war.

Our mornings were sleepy
and slow over breakfast eggs
licking the plate clean
for the sake of others
far away
for Anne Frank
whose eyes looked up at us
from a book cover.

In our starched dresses
we stepped over sidewalk cracks
(not to be the old maid when we got older)
and crouched beneath our school desks
making believe until the sirens
blew the "All Clear."

It was practice just in case the bombs
fell from the sky onto our school.
We clutched our dog tags just in case it was
the real thing and our parents
had to sift through the rubble
to find us.

At recess the girls jumped rope while
the boys shouted "Heil Hitler!"
and goose stepped around
our games. And at night we
climbed into soft beds
dreaming of dolls with red hair
and far away, children burned
in the dark, their eyes melted
but not their bones.

Blue Heron

Years we listened
for the clap of wings
breaking through
the early mist
in the lonely
blue evening
just to watch
for the return:
that flight arched
just above our heads
like a benediction.

Fog

Fog rolls over
my back
like the tide
over sea rocks

Soundless
stone grey
fog
rolls over

the moor-green
rosehip
island
over my eyes

as light thickens
voices groan
on the spine
of tide

fog rolls
over my tongue
listen:

voices
tolling
seatombs

Vanishing Point

The sun warmed green
Pulls taut along the riptide
To a sandy point of gulls:

that edge of earth
where sailors feared to fall
into black space of moons
and fire airless and dry.

Fearless, I step off the shelf
of green descend, the sea's
dark forests through pearls

and silvered fish
descend to cold and night
though the sun burns gold above
as I sleep on a bed of chalked bones

sans desire
forgetting the hum
of plovers' wings

Gaea Speaks

In the ending
light and darkness
will divide
water and dry land
rains will pour from the sky
winds will roil rivers and oceans
winds will raise mighty walls
to crest, swallow grass
and fuit trees
fowl of the air
great whales
cattle of the field
all that creep
upon the earth
and those who had
dominion over all.

Ghost

My mother is already the ghost
of herself lying in this hospital bed.
The skin drapes her bones like a yellowed sheet
that has been laundered too many times. Restless
her grey eyes wander up and down the walls
of the room then come to rest on my face. She
points to her dry mouth and whispers something
I cannot hear as though a great wind were shrieking
at the windows and the drawn blinds rattling
make me deaf and afraid. I give her water
and she closes her eyes to wander elsewhere
haunting empty rooms.

Heaven

Acolyte
of early morning
even today in this biting
cold, my neighbor's
teenage daughter swinging
her heart out in the park
while the town goes
about its business.

This her church.
Her matins.

Back arches, hair flying
like blackbirds,
lips open wide to winter,
a pale moon

waning. She gathers them all
in her eye and works
the air, pumping both legs
all the way.

Homesickness

(for Susanna)

She feels homeless
since he died
not taking her with him
not leaving her entirely

behind. Homesick she visits
other people's houses
lives a while under their roofs
leans against their voices

yet longs to go home
through home is the place
where silence rushes to greet her
washes handprints from the walls.

PART V

Your Life without You

Do you worry your life will end
when you're not paying attention
the way someone steals your wallet
and you don't notice until you reach
for it later just as you're about to pay
for a book of Neruda's poems, then
mumble some apology to the store clerk
before dashing to the commuter station where
you are shoved on the wrong train
and don't notice until you're so far
out of town, it's another country where
an official wearing a mouth like a razor cut
and a dark green uniform demands
the ticket you don't have and you're hauled
to the Office of the Inspector General
who shouts deprecations in Russian and suddenly
you feel like Philbrick in *I Led Three Lives*,
but luckily you hop a train going the opposite
direction and after a few miles, execute
one of those cinematic leaps through the open
window, rolling to safety on a grassy knoll
without breaking both legs, then hitch
a ride home where unaccountably
a Buick is parked out front, another name
lettered on your mailbox, your wife
with some strange man on the couch
watching *Survivor* and neither pays
any attention to you, not even your old dog
who comes in from the dung heap where
he's been waiting all these years
like Argos.

The Blessings of the Grandchild

Even my mother gives up dying
springing out of bed to dance with her:

Ring around o' rosie

Springs in the mattress
bounce on rusty necks

A pocket full o' posie

My father laughs from the dead
where he's been six years

Ashes…ashes
inside my mother's house
all singing

all fall down

October

It happens in a moment
the seam ruptures
branch and stem
the leaves snap off
but the rupture was certain
even at the beginning
that icy April morning
when the sun pries open
each bud sealed tight
as a fist against the cold
and pumped warm sap
through the veins and
suddenly thousands
of pale green hands
waved in the branches
and all summer long
while the birds fussed
in their midst, they drank
the sun with the fury
of things that live
but one season until
the fury burns them alive
and the sparks fly and
smolder on the ground.

Last Light

The violet beneath my mother's eyes
is the color of an iris that holds
onto the last light of day,
that last band of light on the spectrum
before it is invisible as a membrane
separating one life from another
the distance between taking in
the last breath and holding on to it.

Spring

The world is apple green
And you knew it was coming
but still it surprises. A lady bug alights
on your sleeve and you look up:

all the songbirds are returned
from the rain forests festooning
pale trees like party lights

while moths flower beside dandelions
the air buzzes and clicks as a spider
drops from the sky and just as suddenly
a wren carries straw to the eaves of the house

you look at your reflection in a window
and see your mother's face with her look
of surprise and your hair turning grey.

Balancing

(for Emily Age 4)

At Joe's bicycle shop downtown
you choose the rusty one in pink
that matches the bicycle of your dreams.

A silver bell, a helmet in grape
that dips too far beneath your brow.
We drive to the nearest parking lot
to let you have your first ride.

Beneath the helmet you grin your biggest
grin and try with all your might to budge
the stiff pedals that won't budge. We push.
You pedal. We push. At last your legs
propel you far. We cheer
you on.

Those training wheels
keeping all three of us
balanced for a while.

Improvisation

(On a line by Shirley Kaufman)

Sometimes I need to be nowhere
just as I came from nowhere
which astro-physicists say
is the somewhere which was nothing:

not yet this place, as it happens, this earth,
this town ten miles north or south, this street,
this room where I am listening to Schubert's *Last*
Quartets and on the table sits a terracotta vase
cupping one orange day lily which has but one
glorious frenzy.

Interim

i.

Heavy snow fallen
on the kingfisher's nest:
Shiver and snap
of branches
is more than splintering
of wood
      and the swoop
of kingfisher wings
flashing
above a river frozen
to its depths where
also fish abide.

ii.

My daughter bends
to pick the first berries.

Deer graze in a field.

Moments
when the back is turned
the ladder of the spine
exposed, neck cords
stretched taut

between what has happened
and whatever waits.

Keeping Her Company

i.

My mother dies in slow motion
as if she were still mugging
for the old home movies
except the film disintegrates
one frame at a time.

ii.

Is my father calling already?

iii.

Pain sucks her breath
makes her impatient
to go.

iv.

Her sleep is lonely
as my father in his grave
lonely as I am sitting here.

v.

She is lace
unknotting.

vi.

She will leave
only the thread.

What I Would Give Up

I would give up all the words in the world
but not the words that open doors
to unknown rooms.

I would give up all the rooms in the world
but not this room
where I heard music for the first time.

I would give up all the music in the world
but not this music that holds all the light
I have ever seen and all the light I have not.

I would give up all the light in the world
But not this light that makes me reach
For a pencil to write words.

On Your Fifty-Seventh Birthday

for Joel
(July 16, 2003)

Each wave carries you father out
from that first salty cove
to the open sea of storms
where you lose your bearings
and listen for the wail of sirens
to guide you onto the crashing
rocks or you regain direction
in becalmed waters, drift
purposefully like the songs
of dolphins and whales
the poetry of sunlight refracted
on the skeletons of ghost ships
tell the lore of constellations
to the sky, hold the moon in
your arms while beneath the
complexities of currents and
flowering anemone, seaquakes
the lives of fishes, their small
deaths in the dark seabed,
the tide bears you silently
from equinox to solstice
away from the sun once more.

Homesickness

(for Susanna)

She feels homeless
since he died
not taking her with him
not leaving her entirely

behind. Homesick she visits
other people's houses
lives awhile under their roofs
leans against their voices

yet longs to go home
though home is the place
where silence rushes to greet her
washes handprints from the walls.

www.ingramcontent.com/pod-product-compliance
Lightning Source LLC
Chambersburg PA
CBHW032132090426
42743CB00007B/567